ARE WOLVES AFRAID OF THE DARK?

HUW LEWIS JONES
EXPEDITION LEADER

SAM CALDWELL
WILDLIFE ARTIST

CONTENTS

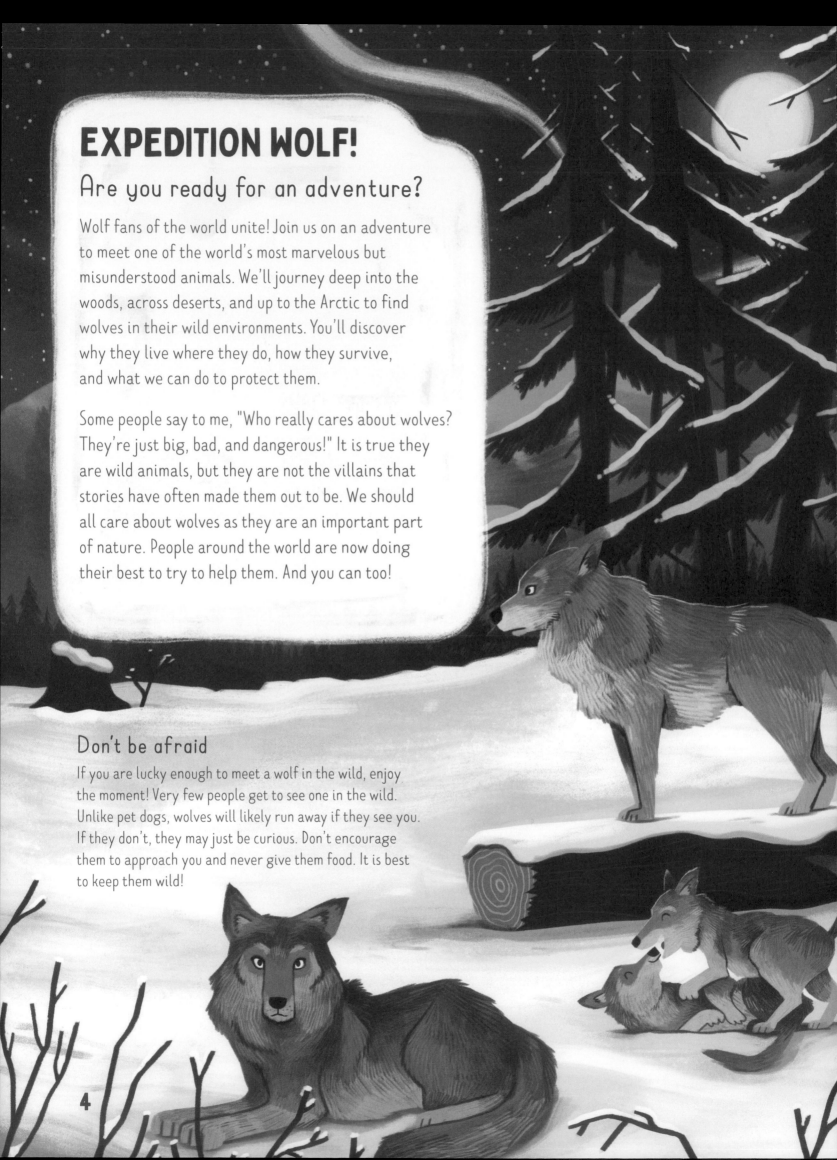

EXPEDITION WOLF!

Are you ready for an adventure?

Wolf fans of the world unite! Join us on an adventure to meet one of the world's most marvelous but misunderstood animals. We'll journey deep into the woods, across deserts, and up to the Arctic to find wolves in their wild environments. You'll discover why they live where they do, how they survive, and what we can do to protect them.

Some people say to me, "Who really cares about wolves? They're just big, bad, and dangerous!" It is true they are wild animals, but they are not the villains that stories have often made them out to be. We should all care about wolves as they are an important part of nature. People around the world are now doing their best to try to help them. And you can too!

Don't be afraid

If you are lucky enough to meet a wolf in the wild, enjoy the moment! Very few people get to see one in the wild. Unlike pet dogs, wolves will likely run away if they see you. If they don't, they may just be curious. Don't encourage them to approach you and never give them food. It is best to keep them wild!

What do I need?

On an adventure what you need most is a brave heart and warm clothes! You can withstand all kinds of weather if you have a good waterproof jacket. Always bring a journal for drawing and writing notes. Binoculars are handy and we often use a spotting scope (a special telescope) to watch animals that are far away. Don't forget a canteen for drinks and a flashlight for when night falls . . .

Wolf wisdom

This book will show you the different types of wolf, the amazing places they live, the foods they eat, and the challenges they still face in our changing world. Wolves are wild animals and it is a privilege to spot them out in nature. We must always respect animals and give them the space they need.

INTO THE WOODS
Would you like to meet a wolf?

If you listen carefully, you might hear a lonely howl in the distance. Perhaps other wolf voices join in and it sends a shiver down your spine. It's an amazing thing to hear and nothing to fear! These wolves are talking to each other. People have been afraid of wolves for thousands of years, but if we try to understand more about them, we might be able to see them a little differently.

Family ties

Wolves may seem scary but they're actually very caring. They live together in large family groups in which teamwork and loyalty are important for getting along. The family bond between wolves is so strong, they would die to protect one another.

Wolves in decline

As more and more people populated the world, many wild places where wolves lived were destroyed. Forests were chopped down and, in many countries, wolves had nowhere left to run. Sadly, habitat destruction still happens today!

Sad history

Around 12,000 years ago, humans started farming sheep, goats, and cows for food. Wolves also relied on these animals for food and left the woods to hunt for them. People started to kill wolves to protect their livelihoods. So began the war against wolves.

Time to thrive

Thankfully, wolves are now making a comeback across Europe and North America. In 1995, wolves were reintroduced into Yellowstone National Park in the United States and have thrived there ever since (see page 40 for more details.)

WILD AT HEART

Where are all the wolves?

Wolves can be found all around the world. They can survive in many different climates, from hot deserts in West Asia to incredibly cold places, such as Greenland and northern Russia. In the past, wolves lived across most of the land in the northern hemisphere. Due to the destruction of their habitat and hunting by humans, they now live in a much smaller area worldwide.

Gray and red

There are two widely recognized species of wolf in North America—the gray wolf and the red wolf. Red wolves are only found in a small area of coastal North Carolina. The main subspecies of gray wolf in North America are the Arctic wolf, the Northwestern wolf, the Great Plains wolf, the Mexican wolf, and the Eastern Timber wolf, which some experts think could be a separate species entirely.

● GRAY WOLVES
● RED WOLVES

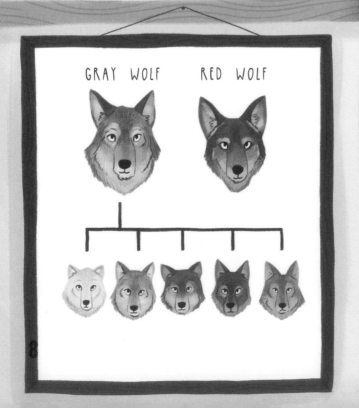

GRAY WOLF   RED WOLF

The great debate

There is still some debate over how many species of wolf exist and how many subspecies of the gray wolf there actually are. Scientists disagree whether in North America alone there are more than twenty subspecies or only four. Confused? It's OK. Some of them are so similar that only a few specialists can tell the difference. They are all amazing gray wolves, that's all you really need to remember.

8

Local names

Wolves are often known by common names that vary across countries and cultures. For example, a gray wolf living in a forested area might be called a "timber wolf" (timber refers to trees), while a gray wolf living out in a remote northern landscape might be called a "tundra wolf" (tundra refers to cold places where there are no trees).

Around the world

There are many subspecies of gray wolf around the world, including the Iberian wolf, which is only found in Spain and Portugal, the Himalayan wolf, which has a thick coat to help it survive in freezing climates, and the Arabian wolf, which lives in the Middle East and is the smallest wolf of all.

KNOW YOUR WOLVES

Do wolves have cousins?

Wolves are the largest members of the dog family, which includes foxes, jackals, coyotes, wild dogs, and domestic dogs.

To find out which members of this family are closely related to each other, look at their scientific names. The gray wolf's scientific name is *Canis lupus*. The first part of the name is the genus and the second part of the name is the species.

If two different species have the same genus, it means they are closely related. All the species pictured here are members of the *Canis* genus!

CANIS LATRANS
(COYOTE)

CANIS RUFUS
(RED WOLF)

CANIS LUPASTER
(AFRICAN GOLDEN WOLF)

CANIS DINGO
(DINGO)

IUCN Red List

Scientists are keeping a careful watch over all species of wolves to make sure they're safe. Look for this symbol on the next page to see which are most in need of our help. There are hundreds of thousands of gray wolves spread across the world, but there are many smaller populations in different countries where they are still threatened.

CANIS AUREUS
(GOLDEN JACKAL)

CANIS SIMENSIS
(ETHIOPIAN WOLF)

CANIS FAMILIARIS
(DOMESTIC DOG)

The gray wolf

The most common species of wolf is the gray wolf. There are more than twenty kinds and they are not all gray! They can be black, brown, tan, and icy white.

CANIS LUPUS
(GRAY WOLF)

Scientific names

Every living thing on Earth that humans discover is given a unique scientific name consisting of two words in Latin, which are always italicized. This naming system is the same all around the world, which helps people who speak different languages talk about animals without getting too mixed up.

GRAY WOLF

Canis lupus

The most common species of wolf.

WHERE? United States, Canada, Greenland, Europe, Russia, and China

HOW MANY? 250,000

LIVES FOR? 6–12 years

IUCN RED LIST STATUS: Least concern

RED WOLF

Canis rufus

Very few of this species still exist. They live in one small part of the USA.

WHERE? North Carolina in the United States

HOW MANY? Only 20–30

LIVES FOR? 6–7 years

IUCN RED LIST STATUS: Critically endangered

ETHIOPIAN WOLF

Canis simensis

The most threatened carnivore in the whole of Africa. More research and protection are desperately needed to help them.

WHERE? The highlands of Ethiopia

HOW MANY? Maybe less than 400

LIVES FOR? 8–9 years

IUCN RED LIST STATUS: Endangered

AFRICAN GOLDEN WOLF

Canis lupaster

These wolves were previously thought to be golden jackals, but we now know they are their own species.

WHERE? Northern Africa

HOW MANY? Unknown

LIVES FOR? 8 years

IUCN RED LIST STATUS: Least concern

DINGO

Canis dingo

These misunderstood creatures most famously live in Australia but there are also some wild dingo populations in Southeast Asia.

WHERE? Australia and Southeast Asia

HOW MANY? 10,000–50,000

LIVES FOR? 7–10 years

IUCN RED LIST STATUS: Least concern

COYOTE

Canis latrans

Coyotes are smaller than gray wolves. They are resilient and live in many more places than wolves do, including urban environments. They seem not to mind humans being close.

WHERE? North America

HOW MANY? 250,000–750,000

LIVES FOR? 6–10 years

IUCN RED LIST STATUS: Least concern

GOLDEN JACKAL

Canis aureus

Golden jackals live in family units and can adapt to survive on all sorts of food, from mammals to fruit.

WHERE? Europe and Asia

HOW MANY? 150,000

LIVES FOR? 8–9 years

IUCN RED LIST STATUS: Least concern

DOMESTIC DOG

Canis familiaris

Dogs evolved from wolves tens of thousands of years ago. They lived closely with humans and became friendlier with every generation. Eventually they became the dogs we know today.

WHERE? Worldwide

HOW MANY? 900 million

LIVES FOR? 10–13 years

IUCN RED LIST STATUS: Least concern

ANCIENT ANCESTORS
Were there dino-wolves?

After an asteroid smashed into Earth 66 million years ago and wiped out the big dinosaurs and many other predators, mammals thrived. Eventually they evolved into a wide variety of shapes and sizes. Long before humans, there were many weird and wonderful creatures, like mammoths, giant armadillos, and even woolly rhinos!

Finding fossils helps researchers learn more about animal history. Fossils of the earliest gray wolves tell us they emerged on Earth about a million years ago. They lived alongside incredible mega beasts, including huge cave bears and saber-toothed cats.

MIACID

CYNODICTIS

Great grand-gopher!
Many biologists believe that the wolf developed from primitive carnivores known as Miacids, some of which were only about the size of gophers. Those creatures first appeared about 52 million years ago.

Dawn-wolf
Relatively late in the evolutionary history of Miacids came the appearance of the first canid, Cynodictis. Some researchers call this the "dawn-wolf." It had a long body and looked a little like a stretched-out fox crossed with a wild cat. It could live in and climb trees.

Dire wolves

In modern-day Los Angeles, archaeologists have found bones of ancient dire wolves. They were big, tough, bone-crunching scavengers that probably lived and hunted in packs, much like the wolves we know today.

SABER-TOOTHED TIGER

DIRE WOLF

EURASIA

NORTH AMERICA

THE GREAT WOLF MIGRATION

Epic crossing

The first true gray wolf, *Canis lupus*, probably appeared in Europe and Asia about a million years ago, during a very long period we now call the Pleistocene. Did you know Europe and Asia were once connected to North America by a bridge made of land, back when sea levels were much lower?

The gray wolf eventually migrated to North America across this bridge. It arrived there a long time before the first people did! The ancestors of North American Indigenous peoples first crossed the land bridge from Asia just 18,000 years ago, when dire wolves still roamed the Earth.

CANINE COUSINS

Are wolves really related to poodles?

It might be hard to believe, but all pet dogs originally came from gray wolves. Yes, even little pugs and curly cockapoos! We think humans started keeping them as companions about 15,000 years ago. Over time they were bred to be friendlier towards humans and became the first animal to be domesticated. Today, dogs are the most popular pets in the world!

Helpful hounds

Humans soon discovered that dogs were helpful for hunting and guarding their homes. Not to mention being fun to play with! Over the centuries, they were bred to be good at different tasks, such as running fast, herding, pulling sledges or carts, and sniffing out and retrieving animals on hunts.

Same but different

Their shared family history has led to similarities between dogs and wolves. They are both social animals that like company. Both have a fantastic sense of smell and use body language and scent marking to communicate. However, they also have many differences. Where dogs are tame and trainable, wolves are wild animals that are likely to be shy and afraid of humans.

Familiar family

The more that dogs were bred, the less and less they resembled wolves. But no matter how different they appear, every dog—from the tiny Chihuahua to the giant Great Dane—is a member of the same subspecies of wolf: *Canis familiaris*.

Playtime

Just like dogs, wolves love to play. They jump, play rough and tumble, and chase each other around. To start their games, one wolf will approach another and pose with its head lowered and butt in the air, inviting them to begin. This is known as a "play bow."

MEAT FEAST

What do wolves eat?

Wolves are carnivores, which means they eat other animals. They are great hunters with excellent teamwork skills and can run for many miles without getting tired. Even so, hunting can be hard, dangerous, and not always successful.

Wolves will eat most things, from mice and rabbits to larger animals, such as deer, elk, moose, and bison. When wolves are really hungry, they will even eat insects, grasses, acorns, or berries. But they would always rather eat meat.

DINNERS FOR ONE

EMERGENCY SNACKS

Hunting party

Working together, a wolf pack can hunt large prey like moose. A lone wolf might have to settle for smaller animals like beaver, rabbits, and rodents, which are easier to catch on their own.

Top dog

Wolves are at the top of the food chain. They are predators, like tigers, bears, and sharks. But remember, little blue tits, and dormice are predators too. Everything eats something else.

FAMILY FEAST

Fishing trip

In British Columbia in Canada, a unique subspecies of gray wolf, known as the sea wolf, lives along the edges of ancient forests that meet the ocean. They spend a lot of time hunting in rockpools and along beaches and mostly live on a diet of marine creatures, such as salmon, octopus, clams, barnacles, and even washed-up whales.

Dinner time?

Unlike us, wolves don't eat breakfast, lunch, and dinner. In fact, they sometimes go days without food. When they do eat, they don't hold back. They can easily eat almost 20 lbs of meat in one meal, which is equal to about 200 hot dogs!

Hunted down

Wolves are afraid of people and rarely attack them. But they do attack farm animals, including sheep and cows. It is mostly for this reason that people have killed millions of wolves over the years.

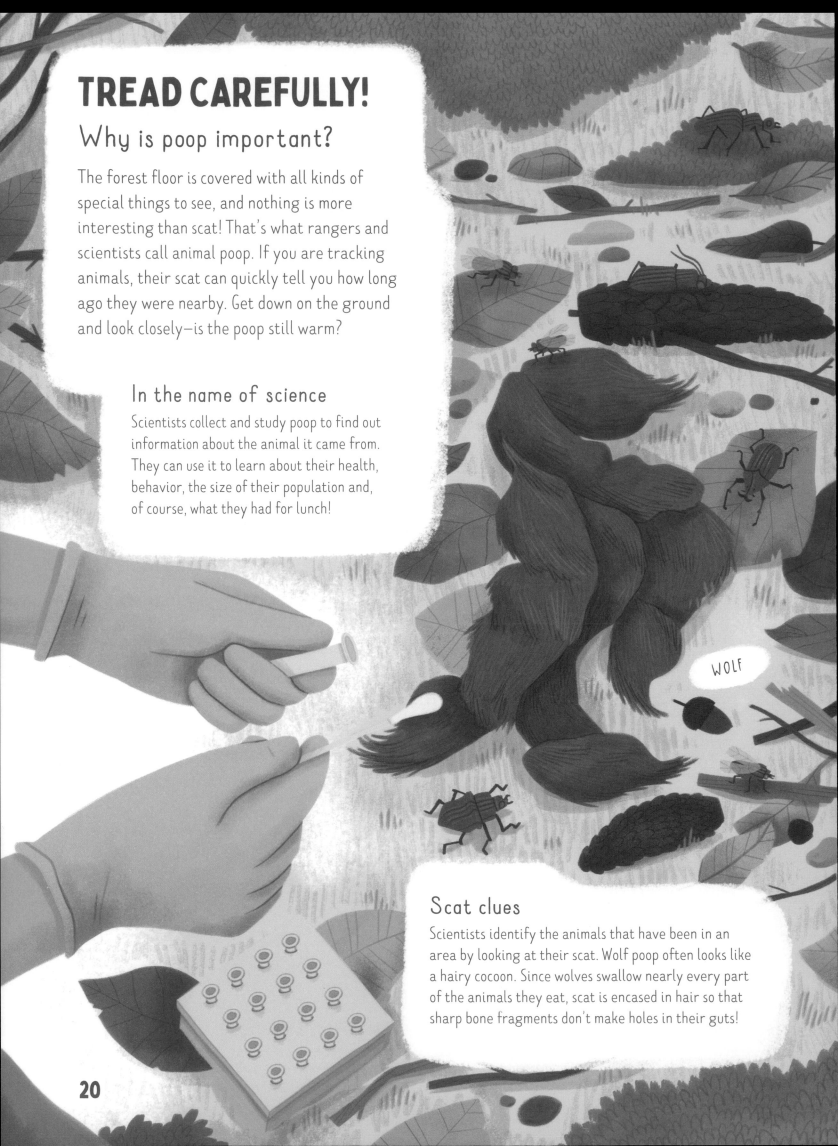

TREAD CAREFULLY!

Why is poop important?

The forest floor is covered with all kinds of special things to see, and nothing is more interesting than scat! That's what rangers and scientists call animal poop. If you are tracking animals, their scat can quickly tell you how long ago they were nearby. Get down on the ground and look closely—is the poop still warm?

In the name of science

Scientists collect and study poop to find out information about the animal it came from. They can use it to learn about their health, behavior, the size of their population and, of course, what they had for lunch!

WOLF

Scat clues

Scientists identify the animals that have been in an area by looking at their scat. Wolf poop often looks like a hairy cocoon. Since wolves swallow nearly every part of the animals they eat, scat is encased in hair so that sharp bone fragments don't make holes in their guts!

Perfect poop

Carnivores that eat lots of meat, such as wolves and lions, make chunky, tube-shaped poops. Wolf scat is usually dark gray and up to 5 inches long, but anyone with a pet dog knows that all shapes and shades are possible!

RABBIT

FOX

WEASEL

MOOSE

Hello there

Wolves sometimes leave their poop in a clear position for others to find easily. It acts like a smelly signpost, to mark their territory and show where they've been. The poop is even more obvious if the wolf has scraped up the nearby soil with its back paws, like dogs do.

WE ARE FAMILY

How do wolves live?

Wolves are very social animals and live together in family groups called packs. Members of a pack need each other to survive. Together they search for food, protect one another, and look after the youngsters. Life can be very hard for a wolf on its own!

Family bonds

Generally, only the top male and female wolves, known as the breeding pair, will have pups, but the whole pack helps to raise them. The top female will usually give birth to one litter of pups a year.

Big and beautiful

The size of a pack can vary a lot. They usually range anywhere between 2 and 12 wolves, but sometimes grow much bigger! The largest pack ever seen by researchers was the "Druid Peak Pack" in Yellowstone National Park, U.S. The pack grew from just 8 wolves in 1999 to 37 in 2001, before they eventually split up to form separate, smaller packs.

Boss parents

Most packs are led by the breeding pair. They are in charge of guiding the pack and making important decisions, like when to hunt, which way to travel, or where and when to sleep.

Better together

A pack normally includes the breeding pair and their pups from that year. Sometimes pups stay for longer, and occasionally they will be joined by a wolf from another pack. Together, they will travel long distances.

23

THE YOUNG ONES
Do wolves care for each other?

Baby wolves are called pups. The breeding female of the pack will usually give birth to between 4 and 6 pups each year, in April or May. When they are born, pups have fuzzy black fur and weigh about as much as a loaf of bread. They are also unable to see or hear. Pups spend their first 2 weeks cuddled up with their mother, until they can open their eyes.

Dig it

For safety and shelter, mother wolves give birth and raise their newborn pups in dens. The most common types of dens are holes dug in the earth, but wolves also use hollow logs or tree trunks, old beaver lodges, and even caves. The same dens are often used year after year.

Good, not gross

Pups drink their mother's milk until they are about 6 weeks old. From then on, adult wolves will return to the den after a hunt and regurgitate food for the pups. It might look like they're throwing up, but they are actually bringing up partly digested meat from their stomach for the young ones to eat.

Tasty toys

Pups are very playful and curious. They will stalk, pounce, chew, wrestle, and play with one another. Sometimes they find a "toy," like a feather or a piece of fur, and will spend hours with it. The pups also practice their hunting skills by learning to catch small animals, such as mice.

Family time

Wolf pups start hunting with the pack at about 6 months old. Until then, each adult takes turns babysitting and teaching them skills as they play. Anytime after their first birthday, wolves can leave their pack to search for a mate and their own territory.

PRESS PAWS

Can you follow these tracks?

A print left by an animal is called a track. Wolf tracks are larger than those belonging to most pet dogs and other canids. Their front paws are bigger than their back ones and their toes spread wide, which helps when traveling through thick snow. An adult gray wolf's front paw is usually about 4 inches long and 3 inches wide.

Whose prints are those?

Forests in the northern hemisphere are filled with all kinds of tracks. Animals like bears, wolves, badgers, otters, and rabbits leave recognizable paw prints. Other animals, such as deer, elk, and moose, leave different shaped tracks with their hooves.

WOLF'S FRONT PAW

RABBIT'S HIND FOOT

DEER HOOF

Tricky to track

Wolves have fantastic hunting skills, which make them very hard to track down. With their excellent sense of smell and sharp hearing, they can sense humans coming from over a mile away. They can also move around a lot, sometimes running 15 miles in a single night.

Feathered friends

Another way to help you spot wolves might be to look up! Wolves are often followed by ravens. In fact, they have a special kind of friendship, known as a mutual relationship. Ravens alert wolves to dangers and feed on what's left after a hunt. Researchers have found that some ravens make their nests near wolf dens, and young pups and birds have even been seen playing together.

Hide and seek

Animal tracks are easiest to see during the winter when the ground is covered with snow, but if it is very thick, the prints only look like deep holes, which makes them hard to identify. At other times, look for places without vegetation, especially after rain when the ground is soft. The best prints are usually found in damp mud, on the beach at low tide, or on banks near lakes and streams.

NIGHT VISION

Are wolves afraid of the dark?

Some people still have nightmares about wolves. Perhaps the wrong kind of bedtime stories are to blame! But I wonder, do wolves have bad dreams too? Just like humans, wolves feel emotions, such as worry, fear, and happiness. New research is helping us understand them better, but how do wolves really feel about the dark? Well, pretty comfortable, I'd say!

Night eyes

Like bears, cats, and dogs, wolves have a special reflective layer on the backs of their eyeballs. It is called the *tapetum lucidum*, and gives them excellent night vision. Yes, wolves have super eyeballs!

Perfectly adapted

Wolves have incredible eyesight. Their bright eyes can detect the smallest of movements in the forest and recognize other wolves from far away, even in the dark. In summer, the pack tends to head out to hunt in the evening and returns by morning, avoiding the heat of the day. In winter, they sometimes hunt in the day as well, in a never-ending search for food.

No fear

Wolves don't have many natural enemies apart from humans. Grizzly bears and mountain lions also hunt at night, but because most wolves are in packs, these other predators don't usually bother them. Although bears might try to steal their kills!

Long journeys

In winter, when there is little food, wolves often roam along frozen rivers and lakes, which is easier than padding through thick snow. Wolves are crepuscular, which means they are most active around dawn and dusk. Packs spend much of the daytime resting, which gives them enough energy to trek many miles when it starts to get dark.

WONDER STUFF

What other superpowers do wolves have?

Wolves have another super-sense in their eyes: magnetic vision! Researchers have found a light-sensitive substance in their eyes that allows them to see Earth's magnetic field, which is invisible to us. It's possible that it acts like an internal compass to help them find their way.

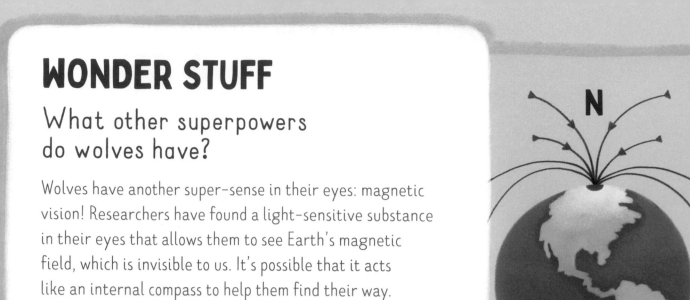

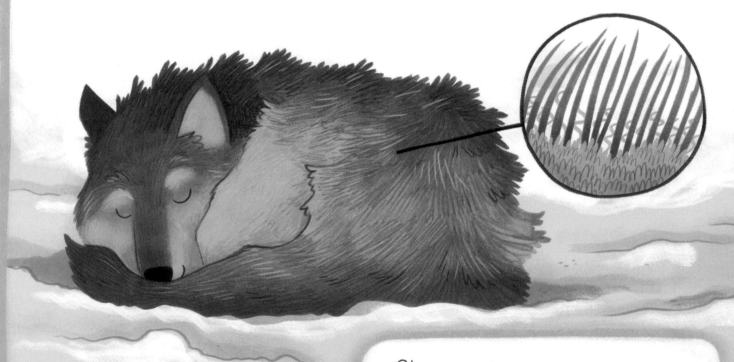

Clever coat

A wolf's coat has two layers. The outer layer is waterproof and made of long, straight hairs. Underneath is a thick layer of soft, downy fur, which traps body heat to keep the wolf warm. Wolves that live in the freezing north have the heaviest coats.

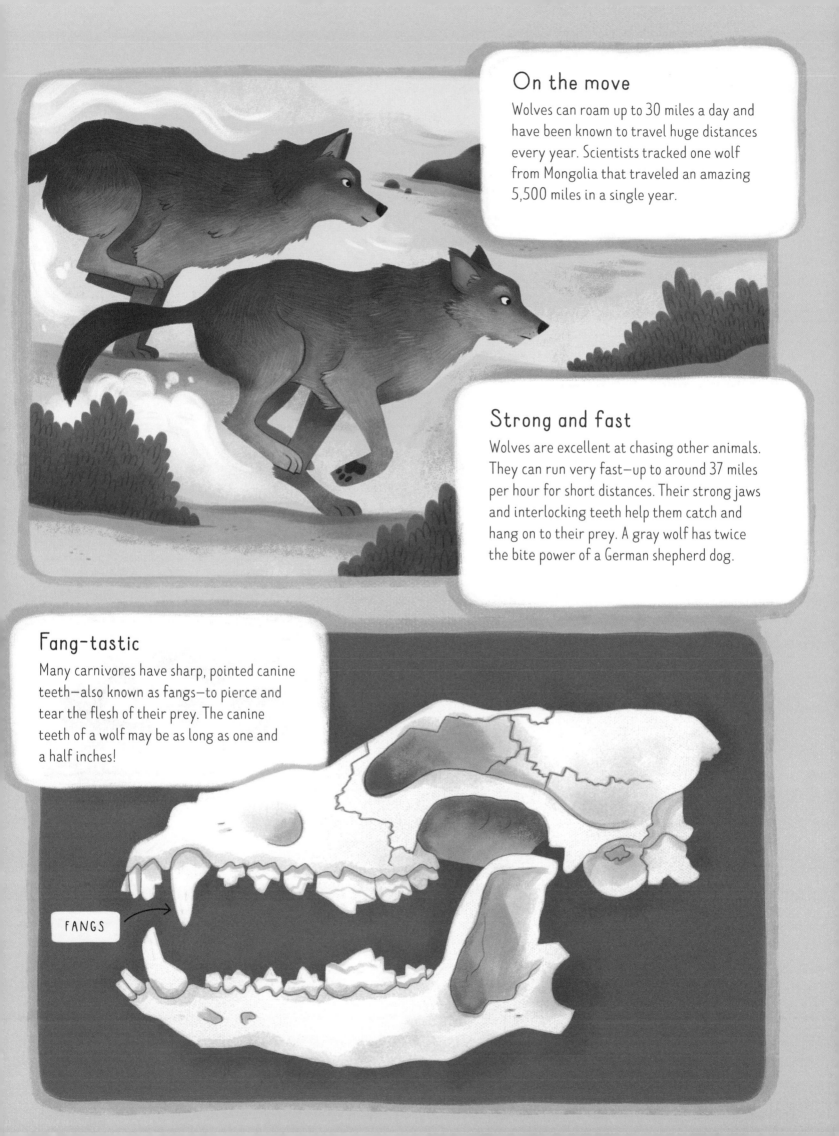

On the move

Wolves can roam up to 30 miles a day and have been known to travel huge distances every year. Scientists tracked one wolf from Mongolia that traveled an amazing 5,500 miles in a single year.

Strong and fast

Wolves are excellent at chasing other animals. They can run very fast—up to around 37 miles per hour for short distances. Their strong jaws and interlocking teeth help them catch and hang on to their prey. A gray wolf has twice the bite power of a German shepherd dog.

Fang-tastic

Many carnivores have sharp, pointed canine teeth—also known as fangs—to pierce and tear the flesh of their prey. The canine teeth of a wolf may be as long as one and a half inches!

FANGS

MOON SONG

Can you speak wolf?

Wolves talk to each other in special ways. It might not sound like anything we would understand, but they are superb communicators. Wolves bark, growl, whimper, and snarl, but they are most famous for their howl! They use it to send messages over long distances and when one wolf starts howling, others often join in. Did you know that sometimes wolves sing just to make music?

This is me

The howl of a wolf is one of the most amazing sounds in nature. It also helps them track the rest of the pack and warn off intruders. To us they might all sound the same, but each wolf has its own unique howl.

To the moon

Even though it might look good in a scary movie, wolves don't really howl at the moon. They howl at each other instead. However, they do lift their snouts towards the sky to howl, because it allows the sound to carry farther. A wolf's howl can be heard for miles!

Good listeners

Wolves have excellent hearing, too. You can see their ears prick up and rotate around to catch faraway sounds. This helps them listen for prey and approaching dangers, but most importantly it helps them listen to each other.

Different voices

Did you know that wolves around the world speak with different accents? Scientists made a study of howling in the canid family, including wolves, jackals, and dogs, and showed that various subspecies had different howling patterns.

STATUS UPDATE

Can wolves understand each other?

Wolves don't only communicate with their voices, they also use smells, body language, and facial expressions. Clear communication allows wolves to care for their young, defend their territory, and work together to hunt much larger prey than they could on their own.

Smell you later

A wolf's sense of smell is a hundred times greater than a human's! They are able to create a kind of map of smells across their whole territory, leaving their scent in specific places for other wolves to find. This is called scent marking and can act as a warning to other packs to keep away.

Pee time

One way that wolves mark their scent is by peeing—scientists call this urination. Both male and female wolves do this. Each wolf's pee smells different, and it's likely that they can tell exactly which wolf left a mark just by having a good sniff!

34

Check me out

Wolves like to pee in obvious spots. Trees, fence posts, and rocks are all good places. You can think of scent marking a bit like invisible graffiti. They use it to say, "I was here!" Wolves also produce scent from glands between their toes, and scratch and spray the dirt to spread their smell around.

Body language

Wolves can use their bodies to say . . .

I'M ANGRY NOW:
Snout wrinkled
Teeth exposed
Ears out to the side

I'M THE BOSS:
Ears pointing up
Tail straight out
Straight legs, standing tall

I'M NOT A THREAT:
Keep low, crouching
Ears flat back
Mouth closed
Tail tucked between legs

WANT TO PLAY?:
Tail wagging
Front paws down like bowing
Butt high

35

TELLING TALES

Are wolves really so bad?

Many of our oldest stories are about wolves. They prowl through our folklore and fairy tales, spreading both wonder and fear. But don't believe *Little Red Riding Hood* or the *Three Little Pigs*! Wolves don't want to eat grandma or blow your house down! They have much more reason to fear us than we do them.

As the number of humans in the world grew, places where wolves had lived for thousands of years were destroyed. More and more, wolves and humans came into contact, which usually resulted in more trouble for the wolves. We must learn how to live together again and rewrite the story!

Saving the day

In ancient Roman mythology, two young twins, named Romulus and Remus, were saved by a female wolf who let them drink her milk.

Creating the world

Wolves are woven into the culture of North American Indigenous peoples. In many stories they are a symbol of intelligence, healing, courage, and loyalty. The Cree believe god-like wolves visited Earth when the northern lights shone in winter. Cheyenne medicine men rubbed warrior arrows against wolf fur to bring success in hunting. Some tribes even speak of a wolf as the creator of the Earth.

Norse myths

In old stories from the north, the god Odin was said to have two wolf companions: Geri and Freki. He would give them all the food from his table, only drinking wine himself. In a final great battle, Odin is swallowed by a giant wolf called Fenrir.

Howling god

To the Ainu people in Japan, the wolf was seen as "Horkew Kamuy," which means the howling god. Ainu hunters would also leave portions of their kills for wolves and treated them with respect.

Shapeshifters

According to myths of some Indigenous peoples, wolves and orcas were creatures with shared spirits. The Yup'ik in Alaska said that they would change back and forth between their two forms at different times of the year.

Bad stories

When a book of *Aesop's Fables* was first published in England in 1484, it contained stories of cunning and hungry wolves, just as real wolves were being hunted to extinction. By 1760 all the wolves in Britain were dead.

TROUBLED TIMES

Will wolves become extinct?

Can you guess what the most dangerous animal on the planet is? Without a doubt it's us! Humans have destroyed more of nature than any other species. Because of us, wolves have become extinct in more than half of the areas where they used to live. Although shooting wolves is now illegal in many countries, the laws are difficult to enforce and many are still killed. We cannot allow these animals to disappear!

FLORIDA BLACK WOLF
LAST SEEN: 1908

The Florida black wolf, a subspecies of red wolf, disappeared as habitats were destroyed and it was hunted to extinction by people who feared for their livestock. They lived near the Indian River Lagoon and liked to eat small deer and rodents. Florida still has black bears and panthers, but wouldn't it be great if wolves were back there, too?

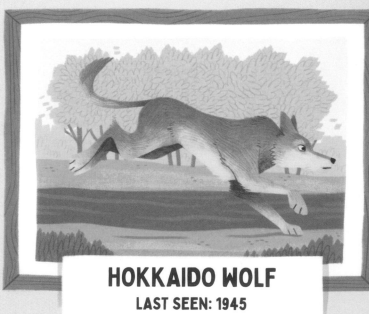

HOKKAIDO WOLF
LAST SEEN: 1945

This extinct subspecies of gray wolf, also known as the Ezo wolf, once lived throughout Japan and eastern Russia. It was seen as a threat to horses and was killed off by farmers, often with poisoned meat left in traps. The last sightings were on a remote island called Sakhalin.

GREGORY'S WOLF
LAST SEEN: 1980

Gregory's wolf is the most recent wolf to go extinct in the wild. It was a slender subspecies of the red wolf that once lived in the swamps of the lower Mississippi River. Its coat was a mixture of black, white, gray, and reddish-brown.

THE RAREST WOLF
LESS THAN 20 LEFT IN THE WILD

The red wolf is the most endangered type of wolf. In 1980 it was declared extinct in the wild, but a captive-breeding program was started to try to bring them back. Now just a handful exist in the wild in North Carolina, but there is hope that one day populations might be able to recover.

Pay attention

Animals that are said to be endangered are very likely to become extinct in the near future, unless we act fast. Endangered animals are at risk because of issues like habitat loss, hunting, pollution, and the climate crisis. Extinction means that all members of a species have died out. This cannot be allowed to happen!

REWILDING

Can wolves thrive again?

By the early 20th century, things were looking very bad for wolves. They had already completely disappeared from many countries and regions around the world, and in others their numbers were dangerously low. This was mostly due to humans hunting wolves out of fear for their farm animals. Thankfully, laws were later passed to protect wolves and today they are returning to many areas.

Packs in the park

Yellowstone National Park in the U.S. was once home to lots of wolves but by 1926 they had been wiped out. In 1995, scientists reintroduced gray wolves into the park from Canada, and they have remained there ever since. This rewilding project has generally been considered a big success, paving the way for more wolf reintroductions in other places. However, wolves that stray outside of the park's borders are at risk of being shot by people who dislike wolves.

Comeback tour

Thanks to protection laws and conservation work, wolf numbers are recovering across much of Europe. Some are even crossing back into countries where they have been missing for a long time, including Denmark and the Netherlands.

Wilderness ways

Wolves are known as a "keystone species," which means that they have an important effect on the natural habitats where they live. When wolves disappear from an area, the numbers of animals that they usually prey on, such as deer and elk, can grow too large. This can lead them to suffer from hunger and disease, as well as the loss of many plants, trees, and other animals from their local environment.

Still hunted

Some parts of the world have laws that continue to allow wolves to be hunted in places where their populations are at risk. Conservation groups are speaking out against this, but people's fear and misunderstanding are still the biggest threats to the survival of wolves.

SUPER SCIENCE

Can technology help wolves?

There are scientific studies of wolves being carried out right now, all around the world. Researchers can learn about the daily lives of wolves by fitting special collars that track their movements. They also take samples of blood and collect poop to better understand their health and feeding habits.

Smart collars

Tracking collars are equipped with different types of technology. Many have a GPS receiver, which sends regular updates of its location throughout the day, to show where the wolf is traveling. Collars also have a device to send text message alerts and a radio transmitter. They can be programmed to release and drop off, as it would be unfair for a wolf to have to keep the collar on forever.

Out of the box

To avoid the risk of causing injury or distress, new techniques are being developed that don't involve trapping the wolves, such as measuring and recording their sounds. One project in Montana is using a remote device called a "Howlbox," which plays howling noises in the forest and then records any responses.

Wonder walk

In 2011 in Slovenia, a wolf that researchers named Slavc was fitted with a tracking collar. In 4 months, he traveled over 1,200 miles, through the mountains of Austria to the farms and vineyards of Verona in Italy. He crossed highways, swam across rivers, and tackled thick winter snow. He eventually met a female wolf, Juliet, and they raised more than 16 pups together.

Wolf's-eye view

In 2021, researchers in Minnesota used a collar with a camera attached to film the world from a wolf's perspective. It recorded footage in 30-second chunks each day through the summer and found that the wolf, named V809, spent a lot of time napping and hunting for fish in the river.

LIVING TOGETHER
Do wolves need some love?

We must learn to co-exist with other animals. Humans can be destructive, but we also have the potential to do amazing things. There are many people around the world trying to save wolves. Protecting habitats is the best way to ensure wild animals have a future.

Give them space

It is time we gave wolves more of our attention and love! But most wild animals don't really want to cuddle with us, they just want to be left alone. We must learn to give animals all the space they need. If we respect nature and protect habitats, wolves will continue to recover. With more wolves, the world will be a happier, healthier, and wilder place!

Wise up

All types of wolves need healthy habitats to survive. Humans are still cutting down forests, polluting rivers, and contributing to climate change, which makes it increasingly difficult for plants and animals to thrive. But it is still possible to help the wolves of the world if we stop trashing our planet.

Busting stereotypes

A stereotype is an opinion or belief that many people share, which is often unfair or untrue. Stereotypes about animals can be found in the expressions we use. Have you ever wondered why we say, "So-and-so is such a chicken," or "a greedy pig," or "sly as a fox?" Can you think of any stereotypes about wolves?

Join in

Fortunately, attitudes towards wolves are changing. We even have special dates to celebrate them every year. On August 13th we have "International Wolf Day," and in North America the third week of October is "National Wolf Awareness Week." You can join in the fun by having your own wolf party or help raise money to support conservation charities.

WOLF WORDS

ARCHAEOLOGISTS: Scientists and historians who study the ancient remains of humans and their cultures.

BODY LANGUAGE: "Talking" with actions, not words.

CANIDS: A family of mammals that includes dogs, wolves, coyotes, and foxes.

CAPTIVE BREEDING: A group of animals that are looked after to help them produce offspring, sometimes for rewilding projects.

CARNIVORE: An animal that mostly eats meat.

CLIMATE CHANGE: Long-term changes in global temperatures and weather patterns. These are caused not only by natural processes but also by human activity, including burning fossil fuels, such as coal and oil.

CONSERVATION: Protecting animals and nature, today and into the future.

DEN: A burrow in the ground or in a cave where wolf mothers give birth and feed their pups.

DOMESTICATED: Animals that have been tamed and kept by humans.

ENDANGERED: May soon no longer exist.

EVOLUTION: The gradual change of a species over time, usually making it better able to survive and reproduce.

EXTINCTION: When a species of animal or plant no longer exists.

FOSSILS: The remains or shape of prehistoric plants or animals, preserved in rock.

HABITAT: The natural environment of animals and plants.

MAGNETIC FIELD: A magnetic force from the center of the Earth, which extends out into space.

MAMMALS: Animals that have hair on their bodies and nurse their young with milk.

POPULATION: The number of animals in the same species that live in a given place, a region, or added up across the whole world.

PREDATOR: An animal that kills or eats other animals.

REGURGITATE: When an adult wolf brings up half-digested food from its stomach to feed its pups.

REINTRODUCTION: Releasing plants or animals back into an area where they used to live but where they can no longer be found.

REWILDING: Giving an ecosystem a chance to become whole again, by releasing plants and animals and allowing the landscape to become wild.

SCAT: Animal poop.

SPECIES: A group of animals or plants that can breed together.

TERRITORY: An area of land where an animal or group of animals live, which they defend from intruders of the same species.

TUNDRA: A vast, cold, flat, treeless region.

INDEX

Be the first to know about our new releases,
exclusive content and author events by visiting
thamesandhudson.com
thamesandhudsonusa.com
thamesandhudson.com.au